John Hegley

A SCARCITY OF BISCUIT

Second Edition: *A Scarcity of Biscuit* by John Hegley.

ISBN: 978 1 7396674 5 0

All poems printed here remain the sole copyright of their author John Hegley, under the Copyright, Design and Patents Act 1988.
No part of this work should be reprinted without the permission of the author.

Cover drawings and those within by and copyright of John Hegley.

First published in the UK 2021 by Caldew Press. This edition published 2022.

Caldew Press
Tolivar
12 St George's Crescent
Carlisle
CA3 9NL

www.caldewpress.com

Printed by Charlesworth Press, Wakefield, UK.

CALDEW PRESS

For Bel, Mel and Marcel.

*John Keats, in a letter to John Hamilton Reynolds
dated Thursday 19th February 1818, suggests we might*

read a certain Page of full Poesy or distilled Prose...
wander with it, and muse upon it, and reflect upon it,
and bring home to it, and prophesy upon it, and dream upon it,
until it becomes stale—but when will it do so? Never.

Acknowledgements

Versions of three of these pieces first appeared in the anthology *Here we go round the mulberry tree*, published in 2013 by London Metropolitan Archives, whose Geoff Pick has been very helpful with this pamphlet.

A thank you to Lilias Fraser for giving a valuable overview of the text and to Rosemary Hill who pressed for drawings to be included. Thank you to Pascale Giudicelli for advising on the French, to Cristina Calò for her Italian translation and to Caldew Press for their warm and patient liaising.

Author details

John Hegley was born in Islington, North London, in 1953 and currently lives in the neighbouring borough of Hackney. He was educated at schools in Luton and Bristol before studying Sociology with European Literature and the History of Ideas at the University of Bradford.

He was the Keats House poet in residence in 2012.

CONTENTS

Celerbration	1
Maureen Roberts Offers the Sanctuary of a Residency at Keats House, Hampstead	2
Rommi Smith's Doctor Poets Workshop at Keats House	2
The Way to Walthamstow	3
From a Conversation With John Keats	4
A Pleasant Prison	5
Northern Souls	6
John Keats on Devonshire Raining	8
John Keats in Scotland	9
For Two Men of Medicine and Poetry	10
C.L.R. James Considers John Keats	11
John Keats on Our Condition	11
Verse Composed Thinking About John Keats While Watching a Toddler on a Lap, on a Swing	11
Knight and Daytime	12
Of an Irishwoman's Life and Sensations	14
Hats and John Keats	18
Una Canzone Per Il Signor Keats	20
A Song for Signor Keats	21
Water and John Keats	21
Paint John Keats	22
Keats, Shelley, Rome 1952	23
A Tree for John Keats	24
Letting-Go of the Fretting	24
A Song for George Keats	25
A Scarcity of Biscuit	26
From Fanny Brawne	27
Cher Monsieur Keats	28
Dear Mister Keats	28

Celerbration

>nothing particular happened yesterday evening, except that when the tray came up, Mrs Dilke and I had a battle with celery stalks – she sends her love to you.
>— *From a long letter to brother George and sister-in-law Georgina Keats, begun 16th December 1818.*

You played the way you worked, John Keats
played hard.
With Mrs. Dilke
with celery
en garde.
On the landing
with your landlady
a new event was marvellously made.
With the greenery
a lunging in, leguminous.
A swish and swash,
a poetry voluminous.
The ballad of a salad day and then:
the celery is mighty as the pen.

Maureen Roberts Offers the Sanctuary of a Residency at Keats House, Hampstead

> I have a swimming in my head – And feel all the effects of a Mental Debauch – lowness of Spirits — anxiety to go on without the Power to do so which does not at all tend to my ultimate Progression – however tomorrow...
> – *John Keats to Taylor and Hessey, his publishers, 16th May 1817.*

I was down in the dumps and the dark
and then Maureen was there with a spark.
She explained I could come
and be John Keats's chum
and how meeting that young man would mark me.

Rommi Smith's Doctor Poets Workshop at Keats House

On the medical side of the man
we focused, with Rommi and Jan
who wore coats that were white
and inspired us to write
and feel better than when we began.

Rommi and Jan Pimblett gave us exercises which were physiotherapy for the muscles of well-being. These included contemplating the plant-life in the peace of the Keats House garden and writing (with dipping-in-ink pens) letters to our younger selves, which we placed in envelopes customised for the journeys across time.

The Way to Walthamstow

John Keats
when he could,
then he would go
to see Fanny, his sister
who lived in Walthamstow:
no North London Line to help him go
on his way to Walthamstow.

As far as we know
as far as he could
he'd take the route which would be taken by a crow
off to see his little sister,
never mind a blister on his toe:
family and poetry
were two such very big ones
to John Keats,
five foot one upon his London feet
and bound for Walthamstow.

One day, on his way to see her
John Keats found a garden centre
purchasing some plants to please her.
In one of his letters to her, he had this to say,
'you did not say a word about your chilblains.
Write to me directly and let me know about them –
your letter shall be answered like an echo.'

John Keats, man of poetry and family and love and nature –
do complain if chilblains give you woe
and, if you're living low on love
then do please let me know
and I will come a-running
or, at least a-walking sprightly
via Tottenham and Hornsey
last stop, Walthamstow.

From a Conversation with John Keats

INTERVIEWER:
So, Mister Keats, as well as the Devonshire rainfall
you had an aversion to Mister Wells, I understand?

JOHN KEATS:
Mister Wells had taken a liberty with my brother
and I took exception. *Me,* they can call a Cockney,
or any name they please, but with my family…

INTERVIEWER:
You expect respect – but, do you respect the French?
You *did* say in a letter to your sister
that the French language is
'the poorest one ever spoken since the jabbering in the tower of Babel.'

JOHN KEATS:
(indignant)
In another of my letters
I speak very positively about the French language for the poet.
In fact, 'Verry good' I call it – with two r's.

INTERVIEWER:
…Something else – Joseph Severn said you told him
you did not believe in his book the Bible.
You said you did not have his faith and hope.

JOHN KEATS:
That is so, but I was glad that *he* had them to help his coping.

INTERVIEWER:
No faith and hope, perhaps, but I believe you had charity –
the greatest of blessings
and you were a fierce defender of your friends as well as your family.

JOHN KEATS:
As I hoped they would defend me.

INTERVIEWER:
Ah, some hope then.

JOHN KEATS:
No faith, though.

INTERVIEWER:
Faith in beauty?

JOHN KEATS:
That's true.

A Pleasant Prison*

The following verse came after reading of John Keats's friend Leigh Hunt being well-treated whilst in gaol, allowed both his dignity and his books. Shortly before that, Napoleonic French prisoners of war kept a sense of self-worth, being permitted to sell outside, items made in their cells. A prison educator once expressed her passion to me for making prison a place of reform and enlightenment. I hope the following verse is in sympathy with her vision and with the liberalism of John Keats.

A men's prison worker, I heard
spoke of duty to blokes we interred
and the good we could add
so the world would be glad
that the lad had been doing his bird.

*A phrase used by John Keats in a letter to Fanny Brawne in the winter of 1820: 'The consciousness that you love me will make a pleasant prison of the house next to yours.'

Northern Souls

John Keats was much taken on his northerly English travels by the Ireby villagers dancing at the Tun Inn, as he would tell his brother Tom on 1st July, 1818.
'they kick and jumpit with mettle extraordinary, and whiskit, and friskit, and toed it, and go'd it, and twirl'd it, and wheel'd it, and stamped it, and sweated it, tattooing the floor like mad'.

We found wonder, in our while under Helvellyn.
We lost our path and found it led to an adventure
and in a tarn, there is a rare fish called the Schelly – what a turn-up!
We've seen the waterfalls
and all the castle walls:
Lancaster and Kendal and Carlisle.
We found wonder, in our while under Helvellyn.

The druid stones, towards Penrith, they drew us in –
they are unlike the Salisbury Plain ones, which have lintels
'on a gentle rise, in the midst of Mountains'*
the druid stones towards Penrith, they drew us in.

William Wordsworth, when we called, he wasn't in –
the story was, he was out canvassing for voters.
I wrote a note to let the poet know 'I was much disappointed'**
(I do hope that the fellow he supports is not appointed!)
William Wordsworth, when we called, he wasn't in.

We saw them dancing at the Ireby village inn.
They kicked up more than just the sawdust and a din,
so different from the French
who tend to dance with buttocks clenching –
don't get me wrong, I'm very fond of very much that comes from France.
We saw them dancing at the Ireby village inn.

To brother George, 27th–28th June 1818
** To brother Tom, 29th June 1818

John Keats composing by 'Druid' stones near Penrith with cat attempting to crunch one of the smaller ones.

John Keats on Devonshire Raining

'The green is beautiful, as they say, and pity it is that it is amphibious.'*
'Devonshire continues rainy'.**
In the following verses, words from John Keats's letters are of the upstanding *type.*

Does it ever rain in Devon?
Does a ten foot wall divide?
Does a dodgem need a driver?
the flowers here wait as naturally
for the rain twice a day
as the Muscles do for the Tide*

Subject to sympathetic moisture*
you'll be rotten cold and drench'd**
Does it ever rain in Devon?
Does Napoleon speak French?

Raindrops to the left of them
the middle and the right of 'em.
the hills are very beautiful,
when you get a sight of 'em***

Letters from Devon to John Hamilton Reynolds, * *14th March 1818 and* ** *9th April 1818.*
*** *To Benjamin Bailey, 13th March 1818.*

John Keats in Scotland

My brother Marcel and I, are sat in the London Metropolitan Archives
reading a letter from John Keats
about his Scottish travels.
Being mischievous for his younger brother, Tom
the poet speaks of 'the horrors of a solo on the bagpipe'.
During our attentions,
coming upon a word in the letter
which we cannot decipher,
on-hand expertise is called in.
Archivist Paul examines and adjudges,
'I think it says *romantic*...
He hasn't crossed the 't' – ROMANTIC!'
The eyes of colleague Maureen
see the word otherwise.
'...*common,* it's COMMON.'
Such are the conclusions of their excellent immersion.
Of course, John Keats had a touch of both:
he was a romantic commoner
(with a bagpipe aversion.)

*In his letter of July 1818 to Benjamin Bailey, John Keats expresses
gratitude to one of the* 'yound' *of the country, who volunteered
assistance to him and his travelling companion, Charles Brown.*
'The People are all very kind. We lost our way a little yesterday and
enquiring at a Cottage, a yound Woman without a word threw on her
cloak and walked a Mile in a missling rain and splashy way to put us
right again'.

A Scot took John Keats for a mile
though the heathery weather was vile;
going out of her way
on that dread, drookit day
for the pay of a wet poet's smile.

For Two Men of Medicine and Poetry

'Hearken thou craggy ocean pyramid'
John Keats's opening line in his sonnet 'To Ailsa Rock' – which stands off Scotland's westerly coastline, sent to brother Tom, the day before arriving in Ayr.

It was on the road to Stranraer, I passed
the shock of rock so rare, which John Keats wrapped
in fourteen lines – its surge, emerging vast
as he considered how this monster slept
half in, half out of ocean – head held high.
The rumbled earthquake giant to him spoke
and what a line it was, with which he was to open his reply
   to this immensity
which I would see, sat on the bus coming from Ayr
where myself and Irfan Merchant had discussed
with coffee he'd provided,
the time of my departure and the fare.

Irfan, I hope, one day I can provide us with another bevvy
as I recite complete, John Keats's ode to Heavy.

```
'I thought you'd be better at drawing horses,
   didn't your dad run a stable, John?'
 'It's a camel, Charles.'
```

C.L.R. James Considers John Keats

The lines below were composed after seeing C.L.R. James on an Arena television programme from the 1985 BBC series Caribbean Nights, made available by Speaking Volumes Live Literature Productions.

Mister James saw the Nightingale ode
as the poet presenting in code,
the upheavals in France
and the flight of the chance
of a more revolutionary road.

> *John to George and Georgina Keats, 17th to 27th September 1819, considering an effect of the French Revolution.*
> 'It put a stop to the rapid progress of free sentiments in England; and gave our Court hopes of turning back to the despotism of the 16th century. They have made a handle of this event in every way to undermine our freedom'.

John Keats on Our Condition

'Call the world if you Please "The vale of Soul-making". Then you will find out the use of the world'.
In a letter to George and Georgina Keats, written over April and May, 1819.

John Keats felt we don't start out whole
what we do is develop a soul,
from whatever we learn
in the trice of our turn
in the ways of the maze and the dice-roll.

Verse Composed Thinking about John Keats while Watching a Toddler on a Lap, on a Swing

John Keats never had any kid.
If he'd had them,
I'd think that he did
                never mind be polite
and them getting words right,
just get love out from under your lid.

Knight and Daytime

Written while contemplating discussing with Sea Mills primary school children in Bristol the painting in the city's art gallery by Sir Frank Dicksee, which is inspired by John Keats's poem 'La Belle Dame Sans Merci'.

John Keats wrote his poems with quills
but, can still hang his coat in Sea Mills,
in the Primary School
making use of a tool
of exceptional rhyme-travel skills.

The knight has a story to tell
about being put under a spell
by a merciless dame
but for her, it's the same:
she is stuck in the story as well.

In the letter of 16th May 1817, to publishers Messers Taylor and Hessey, John Keats considers the 'valiant Knight' *called upon to combat* 'the Fiend', 'the Monster', 'the horrid Propensity' *and suggests engagement without weapons or armour.*
In a letter later that month to Jane Reynolds he speaks of danger being thwarted, merely by 'the armour of words and the Sword of Syllables'.

```
'Right, my faithful horse — I am going to enchant
 the dreadful dragon with poetry.'
'But, Sir, the dragon has flaming breath, razor-
 like teeth and an incredible temper.'
'Yes, my dear friend, and I have some very inter-
 esting poems.'
```

Of an Irishwoman's Life and Sensations

In a letter to younger brother Tom, dated 9th July 1818, John Keats describes the short trip to Ireland with Charles Brown, where they encountered an older woman conveyed in 'the worst dog kennel you ever saw placed upon two poles from a mouldy fencing'. *She seemed to be* 'half starved from a scarcity of Buiscuit in its passage from Madagascar to the cape, – with a pipe in her mouth...'. *The poet muses,* 'What a thing would be a history of her Life and sensations'. *There follows a response from within the kennel.*

My history is blustery;
the winds of change came after me,
I used to be a beauty
but in truth, that time is past.

They used to break their hearts for me,
to move up in their carts for me
and now, this cart I'm carried on
it may not look so solid
and I *may* come over squalid
but, this kennel's built to last.
A carpenter, my father once.
At school, I may have been a dunce
but still, I learned my father's trade
and later on, the carts
in which they'd move up to make room for me
would be
the very ones I'd made.
Be strong inside.
There is a song inside.
The ride it may be rough
but still, inside there is a song.

It's well constructed what you see;
it is a freehold property,
much sturdier than words may think
it stays afloat, it doesn't sink.
It has crossed the channel more than once.
At school, I may have been a dunce
but *not* in woodwork, metalwork and technical drawing.

The shortage of the shortbread is a lot.
The gingerbread is something that is not.
On my narrow shelves, there rests
    no sweet digestive
but, as I pull upon this piping
I will sometimes sense a genie;
a phantom, insubstantial in the mist
with something thin and crisp and fruity
    in her fist.

The leakages are very few:
it's made of teak and ash and yew
but, never mind the flashy stuff,
the *ordinary* is enough:
the time I spend cooking a cake,
a sunflower kissed, beside the lake
another day being awake
a lesson learned by my mistake,
the magpie cackle in a tree
the crust of apple pie for tea
the *filling* of the apple pie
the throttle of the bumble bee
the sticklebacks, the honeysuckle,
I don't hope my luck'll change
it suits me, this arrangement.

Be strong inside.
There is a song inside.
Even living in a kennel,
still inside, there is a song.

My girls and I, we have a gift:
the picking up of languages
the way we pick up wayfarers
who ask if they may have a lift.
It's possible that as I move
around the world, it yet may prove
the old language of love is one
I'll get to speak again.
It almost happened recently, in Spain.

The main thing is, I'm in control
but, as you have suggested
we're extremely low on buiscuits
so, before you travel on your way
could you please say us a poem
and while we enjoy the poem
could you spare me a fig roll?

I'm in cahoots with these two girls

I'll never win an Oscar

But, I'll act as though the world's my oyster

full of pearls and wisdom — and it is, my Pet!

I'll get to Madagascar, yet.

Hats and John Keats

> we walk'd together th[r]ough the Poultry as far as the hatter's shop he has some concern in. He spoke of it in such a way to me, I though[t] he wanted me to make an offer to assist him in it. I do believe if I could be a hatter, I might be one.
> — *In a letter of 1819 to brother George and sister-in-law Georgina, speaking of Mr. Abbey, his sister Fanny's guardian.*

John Keats, once in a natter
said he could have been a hatter
had there been something the matter
with the poems that he made
and the nearest hatting town to John was Luton
so, he could have gone
up northwards from the city
if he couldn't do his ditty,
from the writers' block,
to the hatters' block,
to the Chiltern Hills,
from the Milton skills,
from the sonnet to the bonnet
and the millinery trade.

INTERVIEWER:
So, you knew him as a hatter?

HATTER:
He sat hatting on the bench with me.

INTERVIEWER:
And, was he very handy at it?

HATTER:
He would do his best...

INTERVIEWER:
...but it was best that he went back to the poetry.

HATTER:
He was conscientious – but a conscience doesn't help you
when a hat has to be made.

INTERVIEWER:
So, what was it that got him back to poetry?

HATTER:
Someone in the factory was getting wed
and they asked if he could provide a poem
to be read out on the day?

INTERVIEWER:
And he wrote them one?

HATTER:
He *found* them one – by a mate of his.
But, the couple didn't take to it
so he promised he'd make up one
they could understand.

INTERVIEWER:
And then the muse was back?

HATTER:
No, it wasn't yet – after the wedding
he came round to ours for tea
and made up rhymes for all our children.

INTERVIEWER:
And that was it?

HATTER:
That was nearly it.
Nearly – what did it, was one of them saying,
'Here, Mister – you should make up rhymes for a job
because my dad says when you're making hats
you're totally useless.'

BOTH:
But, conscientious.

Una Canzone Per Il Signor Keats

Beside the Spanish Steps in Rome, a song from a minstrel in the square is addressed to the poet, kept in rooms at the foot of the steps, in hope of convalescence.
The Italian is by Cristina Calò.

Tu sei lassù malato, ed io sono giù in strada.

Io sono un menestrello, devi sentirmi dalla finestra.

Vorrei la mia canzone fosse per te una cura...

Non scalerò l'altura che ho di fronte, fino a te.

Suono e canto quaggiù in piazza di Spagna

mentre tu riposi nella tua stanza.

Il mio cane è qui con me mentre tocco queste corde,

do ali alle parole perché volino da te.

E come il mio cane è un compagno fedele,

spero la mia canzone ti accompagni nel bene.

Io sono una realtà che puoi sentire, mai vedere.

Non avrai niente da spartire con la mia anonimità.

C'è una forza dentro che ci tiene a galla,

accada quel che accada.

A Song for Signor Keats

You are sick and I am in the street, below.
I am a minstrel, you must hear me from your window.
I hope there is a medicine my melody can do.
I will not tread Italian steps that lead to you.

I sing and play across the square, just within sound
while you are there receiving care from those around.
My hound is here beside me as I play upon my strings;
I want my words to come to you, I give them wings –
and as my little dog is faithful unto me
I wish my song to you, a good companion will be.

I am someone you may hear but never see.
You will not share this stranger's anonymity.
There is a strength inside, keeping us afloat
whatever tide it is that takes us.

Water and John Keats

John Keats lived in London, on clay
which made many a brick in his day
but the drainage was poor
as John Keats was – but more,
he made poems where people could stay.

To Naples, then Rome, with the aim
of a hot-headed healing, he came
but the fever was lit
and then following it
was a name writ on water, in flame.

Paint John Keats

Soon after the death of John Keats, Shelley produced Adonais in defence of his fellow poet and attacking a particularly vicious critic of Keats. There follows an imagining of Shelley urging Joseph Severn to paint a last celebratory image. It may be sung to the tune of 'Ain't She Sweet'.

Paint John Keats
for the critics and the creeps,
an antidote to the nasty notices –
Paint John Keats.
Paint John Keats,
standing proud of all his feats:
every inch of all that not that much of him.
Paint John Keats.

Maybe, depict him up in Scotland,
with his apothecary's bottle and
him stood beside some heaps
of celery and 'neeps
with a surgeon's knife, to slice them up with,
will you paint John Keats?

Paint John Keats
in a kilt, with well-pressed pleats;
up in heaven,
Joseph Severn – paint John, will you
Paint John Keats?

*Joseph Severn did paint further portraits of his friend,
but many years after Shelley also had departed.*

Keats, Shelley, Rome 1952

English poet, Christopher Logue visited the resting places of his countrymen with Scottish poet W.S. Graham, who Christopher said looked like a sailor. In the work of W.S. Graham there are many descriptions of the sea, including 'the continual sea' *and* 'the ever Arriving sea'. *John Keats with his own spelling, mused in Margate, upon* 'the reastless sea'.

To the graves of Keats and Shelley
on Italian mainland
two more, from their island went forth.
Christopher Logue from the southerly side
Sydney Graham, more tall, from the North
who would write
of a night and a boat and a fishing
and make many a note of the turns
of the tide.
In his own turn,
his English companion
had once heard spoken
John Keats's nightingale ode
when a smaller salt water
was cried.

A Tree for John Keats

> On arriving at this treeless affair...
> — *To Leigh Hunt, from Margate, 10th May 1817.*

John Keats stayed in Margate, in Kent
and suggested in letters he sent:
there is plenty of sea
but an absence of tree
so for he, I will try to invent one.

T he one I used to get conkers from.

R aided it with sticks sent spinning.

E yes greedy on the tumble down.

E n j o y m e n t of the fruity booty
              later on
                in the
                play
     g r o u n d.

Letting-Go of the Fretting

> I have pass'd my time in reading, writing and fretting –
> the last I intend to give up and stick to the other two.
> — *John, to George and Georgina Keats, early in a long letter of 17th to 27th September 1819.*

The worms of the worry would slink
and cause John Keats's spirits to sink
from the muse and the mirth
'til he opened the earth
and said, 'this is more you, don't you think, Lads?'

A Song for George Keats

My name is George, I'm the brother of John.
I've gone to America and he's just gone.
He was the one, with the questing quill –
the only thing that I ever wrote was another bill.
I'm in the Western Wild, I'm in the Bronco land
where the prairie's wide and the Canyon's Grand.
He filled his pot
with poetic gold
and he got so much, but he didn't get old.
He qualified as a medicine man and he kept on dispensing
with his poetry and his letters to me
and his celery sword fencing.

Now, Mr Shelly, he said John's the one.
But, John – he was never too sure of himself
even though he had the poetry crown on.
I've read some of his verses with a certain difficulty,
but my brother John was easy company.

When we were London children
on the eastern side of town,
every hat John fitted on
it seemed like it was crown jewellery.
He wasn't scared of a schoolyard scrap
with the highest and the hardest chap –
the bigger, the merrier;
what a little terrier!

You didn't have long John.
You didn't have long,
a quarter of a century
and then, you were gone.
You didn't have long John, you didn't have long
but your star shines bright
and your light goes on.

A Scarcity of Biscuit

Standing on the landing, there's a dodo in my home.
I don't know how it got in here; I am on the telephone.
Says the dodo, 'Quasimodo was a bell-ringer, I've heard
and if I had a dead-ringer, then I wouldn't have to be
the only bird of my kind.
I wouldn't have to stand alone.
Get off the telephone!'
I do as I am bidden with a quick apology
to my accountant on the telephone;
the dodo says to me,
'I am feeling rather hungry, have you any custard creams
or even Viennese fingers?'
I take my biscuit packet, tip the contents on the floor.
The dodo eats the lot and says, 'Have you got any more?'
When I explain, the cupboard's bare
the dodo says, 'Let's dance.'
I am up out of my armchair; I appreciate the chance.
Do dodos fly?
I don't know – but I'll find out this one can
and as I hold open the window
I am told the creature's flight plan:
'I am heading for Mauritius.
The provisions were delicious.
The loneliness can be so vicious.'
Before the bird goes from the window
and I wave it on its way,
I have to tell the dodo,
'May you never have to say
I am bereft of a biscuit.
I hope they have left you a biscuit.
Maybe a coconut biscuit?'
The dodo answers,
'Very soon, I'll have to disappear;
do try to remember me
so that you know I was here.
Be strong inside,
where you belong, inside:
there may be no biscuit in the basket
but, inside there is a song.'

From Fanny Brawne

I'm Fanny Brawne
John Keats was torn
from my side; I have cried for the waste.
Now, I see why he
and his poetry
would endeavour
for ever, in haste.

So, we would fail
to build the gaol
where our debt to each other was paid.
If he'd stayed in this life
then a husband and wife
this young Cockney and I
would have made.

Cher Monsieur Keats

Depuis l'autre côté de la mer, j'écris cette carte postale pour vous remercier pour une chose qui nous a apporté beaucoup de joie à mes voisins et à moi-même: c'est votre combat avec le sabre en céleri en branches. C'est l'inspiration pour ce que nous avons appelé 'Les Jeux olympiques des Légumes.' Nous avons *Les Végétaboules*, *Le Billard avec les Choux de Bruxelles* et nous aimons particulièrement *Le Lancer du Fenouil de la Niche* – dans cette épreuve, un athlète dans une niche lance le fenouil et un autre l'attrape dans un entonnoir.
Vive vos jeux, vos mots, vos jeux avec les mots – vos inspirations,
un Admirateur.

Dear Mister Keats

From across the sea, I am writing this postcard to thank you for something which has brought a lot of joy to my neighbours and myself. It is your battle with swords of celery. It is the inspiration for what we have called 'The Vegetable Olympics'. We have *Vegetaboules*, *Billiards with Brussels Sprouts* and we particularly enjoy *Flinging the Fennel from the Kennel* – in this event an athlete in a kennel flings the fennel and another with a funnel tries to catch it.
Long live your games, your words, your games with words – your inspirations,
an Admirer.

```
         Flinging the Fennel from the Kennel
          (into the Funnel, using a Flannel)
```